IT'S TIME TO EAT SQUASH

It's Time to Eat SQUASH

Walter the Educator

Silent King Books
A WhichHead Entertainment Imprint

Copyright © 2024 by Walter the Educator

All rights reserved. No part of this book may be reproduced in any manner whatsoever without written per- mission except in the case of brief quotations embodied in critical articles and reviews.

First Printing, 2024

Disclaimer

This book is a literary work; the story is not about specific persons, locations, situations, and/or circumstances unless mentioned in a historical context. Any resemblance to real persons, locations, situations, and/or circumstances is coincidental. This book is for entertainment and informational purposes only. The author and publisher offer this information without warranties expressed or implied. No matter the grounds, neither the author nor the publisher will be accountable for any losses, injuries, or other damages caused by the reader's use of this book. The use of this book acknowledges an understanding and acceptance of this disclaimer.

It's Time to Eat SQUASH is a collectible early learning book by Walter the Educator suitable for all ages belonging to Walter the Educator's Time to Eat Book Series. Collect more books at WaltertheEducator.com

USE THE EXTRA SPACE TO TAKE NOTES AND DOCUMENT YOUR MEMORIES

SQUASH

It's time to eat squash, oh what a treat,

It's Time to Eat Squash

A veggie so yummy and fun to eat!

It's orange and yellow, sometimes even green,

The prettiest colors you've ever seen!

We cut it in slices, so round and bright,

Or bake it up golden for dinner tonight.

It's soft on the inside, so warm and sweet,

A cozy delight you're happy to meet!

Spaghetti squash strings like magical hair,

You twirl it with forks, it's pasta, I swear!

Butternut's creamy, it's perfect to mash,

A bowl of its soup is gone in a flash!

Acorn's a favorite with its nutty taste,

A sprinkle of spices? There's none to waste!

Roasted in wedges or stuffed like a boat,

Each bite makes you happy; you'll want to gloat!

It's Time to Eat

Squash

Pumpkins are squash too, they love to shine,

In pies and in soups, they're simply divine.

We carve them for faces, we toast their seeds,

A pumpkin's a friend who meets all your needs!

Squash grows on vines, so twisty and strong,

It sleeps in the sun all summer long.

Come autumn it's ready, we pick it with care,

A garden-grown treasure beyond compare!

You can bake it or steam it or grill it up hot,

You can season it lightly or spice it a lot.

Whatever the way, it's bound to be great,

Squash is a star on everyone's plate!

So pick up your fork, take a big bite,

Taste all the flavors, both bold and light.

Eating your squash will help you to grow,

It's Time to Eat Squash

It's good for your body, that much we know!

Now let's give a cheer for this veggie so fun,

Squash is for everyone under the sun!

With every last bite, let's all repeat,

"Oh, squash is so tasty, it's my favorite treat!"

It's fun to explore all the squash you can find,

Each one is unique, with its own design!

From tiny pattypan to big kabochas too,

It's Time to Eat

Squash

There's always a squash that's perfect for you!

ABOUT THE CREATOR

Walter the Educator is one of the pseudonyms for Walter Anderson. Formally educated in Chemistry, Business, and Education, he is an educator, an author, a diverse entrepreneur, and he is the son of a disabled war veteran. "Walter the Educator" shares his time between educating and creating. He holds interests and owns several creative projects that entertain, enlighten, enhance, and educate, hoping to inspire and motivate you. Follow, find new works, and stay up to date with Walter the Educator™

at WaltertheEducator.com

www.ingramcontent.com/pod-product-compliance
Lightning Source LLC
LaVergne TN
LVHW010411070526
838199LV00064B/5261